Small World

Brandon Robshaw

Published in association with The Basic Skills Agency

Hodder Murray

A MEMBER OF THE HODDER HEADLINE GROUP

Photo credits:
p.iv Michael Palin © Basil Pao, Ewan McGregor and Charley Boorman © Steve Finn/Getty Images; Alicia Hempleman-Adams © PAUL GROVER/PA/EMPICS; p.9 © Sipa Press /Rex Features; p.27 © Johnny Green/PA/EMPICS

Orders: please contact Bookpoint Ltd, 130 Milton Park, Abingdon, Oxon OX14 4SB. Telephone: (44) 01235 827720. Fax: (44) 01235 400454. Lines are open 9.00–6.00, Monday to Saturday, with a 24-hour message answering service. Visit our website at www.hoddereducation.co.uk

First published in 2006 by
Hodder Murray, an imprint of Hodder Education,
a member of the Hodder Headline Group
338 Euston Road
London NW1 3BH

Impression number	10 9 8 7 6 5 4 3 2 1
Year	2010 2009 2008 2007 2006

Cover photo © Stuart Redler/The Image Bank/Getty Images
Maps supplied by Barking Dog Art
Typeset in Palatino by SX composing DTP, Rayleigh, Essex
Printed in Great Britain by CPI, Bath

A catalogue record for this title is available from the British Library
ISBN-10: 0 340 91546 3
ISBN-13: 978 0340 915 462

Contents

Michael Palin in the Sahara Desert.

Ewan McGregor and Charley Boorman.

Alicia Hempleman-Adams.

Introduction – Small World?

The world is not really small.
It's big.
It's very big.
It's over 38,000 kilometres
all the way round.

It has five great oceans.
It has seven huge continents.
It has over 150 countries.

So it's not really small at all.
Yet one person can see quite a lot of it
in quite a short time.

This book is about four travellers.
They made three great journeys
in just a few weeks.
They travelled
thousands and thousands of miles.
They proved that,
if you have the time and the energy,
you can make this great big world
seem quite small.

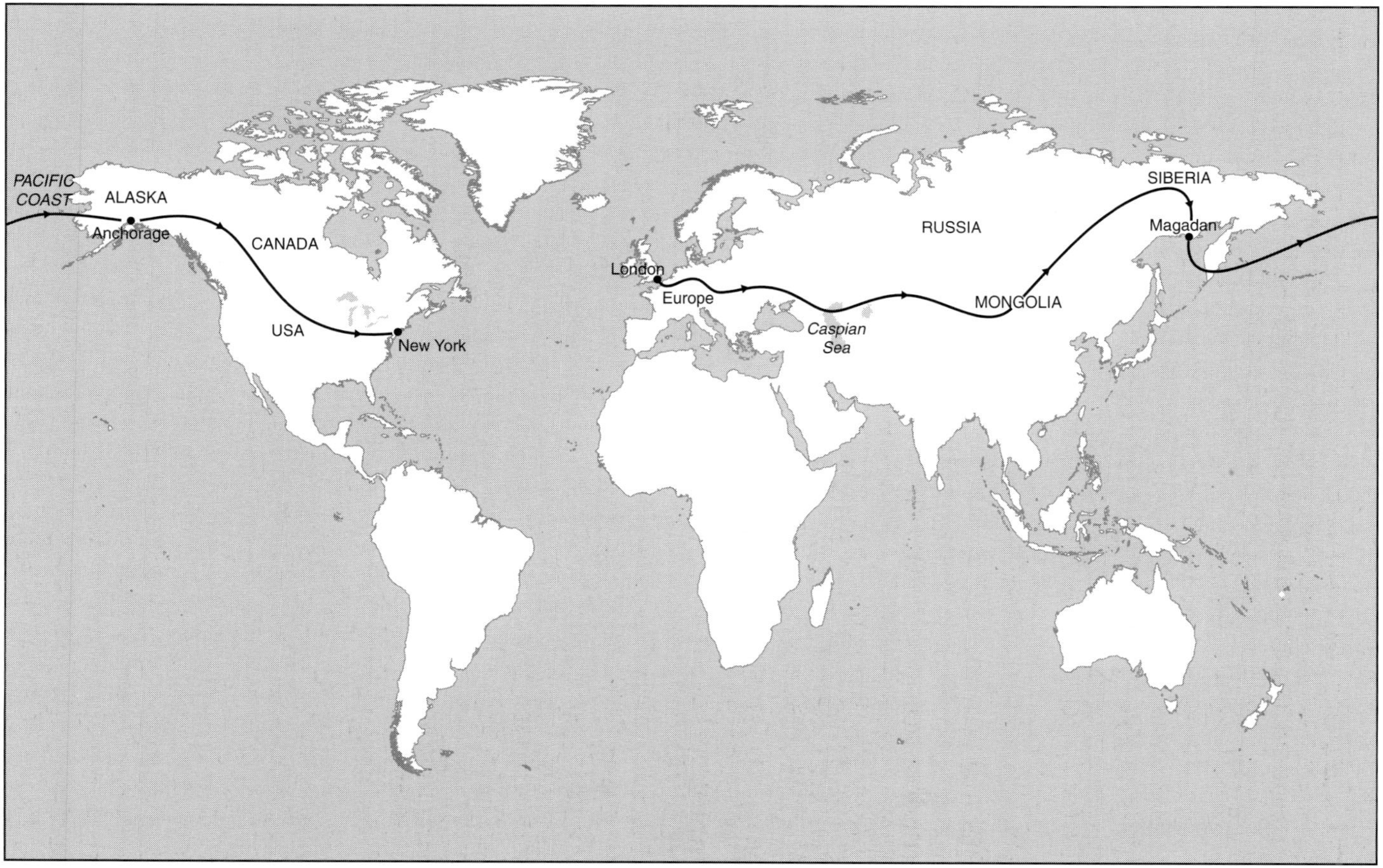

Map of the journey taken by Ewan McGregor and Charley Boorman.

Part One

1 London to New York – by Motorbike!

One way to see a lot of the world
is by motorbike.
What if you got on a motorbike
and just set off in a straight line?
Ewan McGregor and Charley Boorman
did just that.

Ewan and Charley are both actors.
Ewan is in the *Star Wars* films.
They are friends – and they both love motorbikes.

One day they had an idea.
They would ride their motorbikes
from London to New York –
going overland nearly all the way.

It seemed a mad idea.
Yet with careful planning,
they knew they could do it.

The journey would be 32,000 kilometres.
It would take 108 days.
They would cross 19 time zones.

They bought two new BMW motorbikes.
They trained in off-road riding.
They learned how to fix the bikes
in case they went wrong.
They took a first-aid course
in case they had a crash.

They planned the route carefully.
They would ride through Europe,
then through Russia,
then through Alaska,
down through Canada and into the USA.

They also hired a cameraman, Claudio,
to go with them.
They were going to make a film of their journey.

On 14 April 2004, they set off
from Shepherd's Bush, London.

After a few kilometres,
they stopped to fill up with petrol.
At the petrol station, Charley's bike fell over.
Not a good start!

2 Across Europe and Russia

Ewan and Charley crossed the English Channel.
Then they rode their bikes
through France, Belgium and Germany.
The cameraman, Claudio, went with them.
He rode a motorbike too.
Just before the journey began,
he had taken his motorbike test –
and failed it!
Yet he turned out to be as good a rider
as Ewan and Charley.

They went through the Czech Republic
and Slovakia.
Things got harder.
They were held up at one border for hours.
At last they were allowed through.

They made friends with a local called Igor.
They drank and sang for most of the night.

All Igor's friends carried guns.
This made Ewan and Charley a bit worried.
But no one got shot!

Then they headed east.
They stopped to fish in the Caspian Sea.

The roads were very bad.
There were no hotels.
They had to camp out every night.
They had to watch out for scorpions
and poisonous spiders.

Once, they had supper with some locals
who gave them a sheep's head to eat.
Ewan ate some, but Charley didn't!

Ewan and Charley with all their equipment on their bikes.

Then they rode through Mongolia.
This was the hardest part of the journey.
There were no roads, just rough tracks.
The ground was muddy, there were bogs,
there were rivers to cross.
They could only do 40 kilometres an hour.

At last they reached Siberia, in Russia.
Here they rode on the 'Road of Bones'.
The Road of Bones was built to go to
the gold-mining towns of Siberia.
Prisoners were sent to work on it.
Many died and were buried under the road.
That is why it was called the Road of Bones.

They had to cross lots of rivers.
They had to put the bikes on a truck
which drove across the biggest rivers.

At last, they reached Magadan,
a town on the Pacific coast.
The hardest part of the journey was over.
Tomorrow, they would take the plane to Alaska.

3 Made It!

The plane took them to Anchorage, Alaska.
It felt strange to be back in a modern city.
The journey had been hard.
Yet in a strange way they missed it.

Ewan and Charley rested for four days in a hotel.
They had the bikes serviced.
Then they set off.

It made a change to ride on good roads again.
The downside was the traffic.
In the wilds of Mongolia,
they'd had the place to themselves.
Here, there were cars everywhere.
Ewan's bike was hit by a car from behind –
he nearly fell off.
If he had fallen, he would have been killed.
He just managed to stay on.

They rode down through Canada
and into the USA.
At last, 108 days after they had started out,
they reached New York.

Ewan and Charley had had some tough times.
There had been danger –
and they had had a few rows along the way.
But the trip had made them
even better friends than before.
As Charley said,
'After a trip like this,
you share something between you,
a bond that you keep between you forever.'

The film of Ewan and Charley's adventure
was a great success.
It is called *Long Way Round.*

Part Two

4 The Sahara Desert

The world has many different landscapes.
There are plains, there are mountains,
there are jungles –
and there are deserts.

The desert is one of the hardest landscapes
to live in.
The biggest desert in the world
is the Sahara Desert, in North Africa.

The Sahara is hot, dry, empty – and huge.
The Sahara is about 1,600 kilometres
from north to south.
It is about 4,800 kilometres from east to west.
That's about the size of the USA.
Only 2.5 million people live there –
less than one person every 2.5 square kilometres.

This is the landscape Michael Palin
went to explore in 2002.

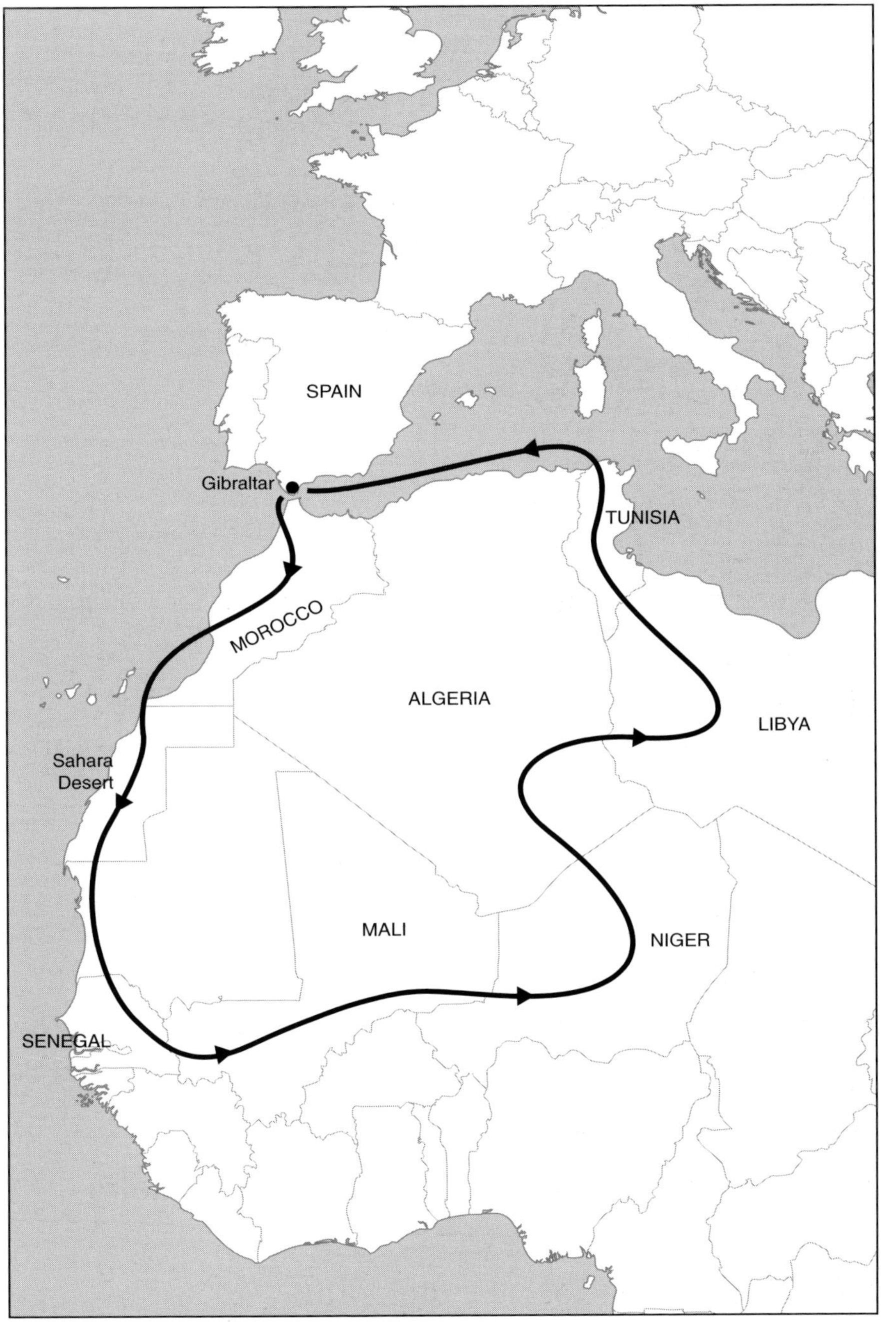

Map of Michael Palin's journey.

Michael had already travelled much of the world.
He had travelled from the North Pole
to the South Pole.
He had gone round the world in 80 days.
Yet his journey through the Sahara
was one of the hardest –
and the strangest.

He travelled all the way down
the Sahara, then across it,
then back up again.
He went by car, by bus
and on the back of a camel.
It took him 99 days.

5 Into the Desert

Michael began his journey at Gibraltar,
off the coast of Spain.

He took a boat to Morocco, North Africa.
He took a bus to the edge of the Sahara.
From here, he and his TV crew
drove into the desert in a jeep.

There are no roads in the desert.
Just sand and rock.
They had to search for firm parts to drive on.

Some parts of the area are dangerous.
There has been war there in the last few years.
Michael spent some time at a refugee camp.
He made friends with the refugees.
They gave him camel's liver to eat.
This gave him an upset stomach!

Michael and his team drove further south.
They reached a 'sand sea' –
miles and miles and miles of soft golden sand,
piled up in dunes.

Driving through sand dunes is very dangerous.
It would be easy for a car to turn over.
It could crash down the slope.
Luckily, Michael's driver knew what he was doing.
He got them through safely.

They went through Senegal and Mali.
In Niger, Michael rode on a camel.
This was the hottest part of the desert.
The temperature was 55°C.
At that heat, the human body loses
nine litres of water a day.
You have to drink water all the time.
If you didn't, you would die.

6 Out of the Desert

Michael and his team turned north into Algeria.
Algeria is in the middle of a civil war.
They had to travel with armed bodyguards.
Michael is good at making friends
wherever he goes.
In one town in Algeria,
he made friends with the Mayor.
He slept on the roof of his house.
The mayor invited everyone he knew in the town
to come and meet Michael.

The next day, Michael was on the move again.
They drove through a rocky part of the desert,
past a range of mountains, 3,000 metres high.

Michael reached the border with Libya.
The border is marked by a single tree,
alone in the desert.
There are sand dunes all around.
Michael said this was one of
the most beautiful places in the Sahara.

The Sahara Desert is a hard place to live in,
but it is very beautiful.
The empty space. The sand dunes.
The mountains.
The sunrises. The sunsets.
At night it is very, very cold
and the stars are bright.

Michael drove through Libya,
then Tunisia, and back to Gibraltar –
then home at last.
The journey had taken 99 days.
A TV series was made of the journey – 'Sahara'.

Michael said he was glad to be home –
but his thoughts still keep going back
to the space and the silence of the Sahara.

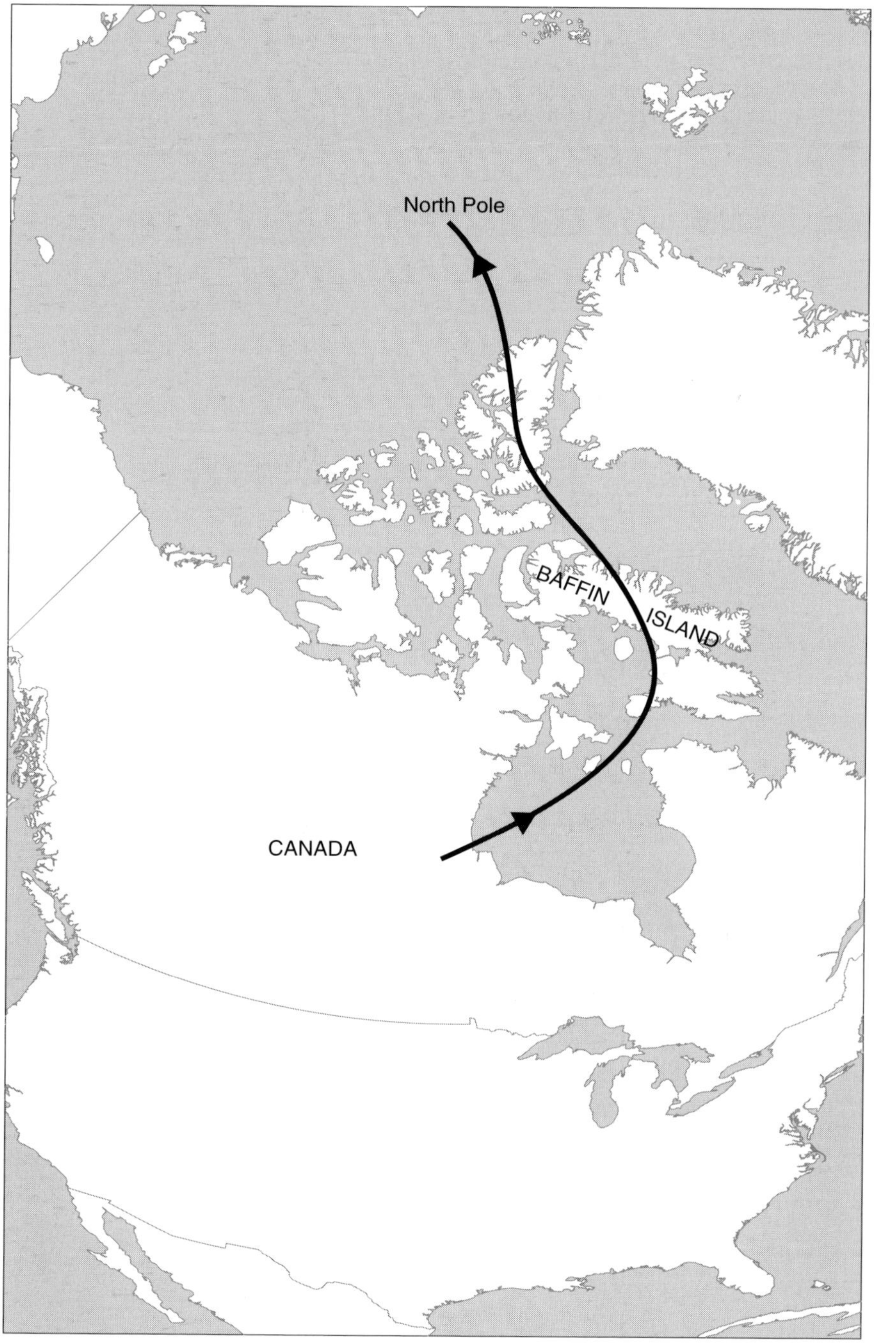

Alicia's journey to the North Pole.

Part Three

7 You Don't Have to Be Famous

You don't have to be famous
to make amazing journeys.
You do not even have to be grown-up.
English schoolgirl Alicia Hempleman-Adams
made an amazing journey.

She was 15 years old
and she went to the North Pole.
Alicia's father is also an explorer.
He has been to the North Pole twice.
At the age of eight, Alicia flew to meet him
at the North Pole.
Alicia was the youngest person
ever to reach the North Pole.

So she already held one world record.
In 2005, she set out to make the journey again –
but this time on foot!
She would be the youngest person ever
to reach the North Pole on foot.

Her journey would take her across Baffin Island,
in North Canada.
It would be a hard journey.
The temperature there can reach –50°C.

Before she went, Alicia trained hard.
She pulled sledges along a beach.
She practised walking with a heavy rucksack.
She practised skiing at an ice rink.

She went with her PE teacher, Jo Simmons.
Before she went, Alicia said,
'It's going to be pretty cold,
but amazing scenery.'

When her 90-year-old great-grandmother
heard about it, she said,
'Oh no, not again!'

8 Reaching the Pole

The journey was 320 kilometres
from north-east Canada,
through snow and ice and strong winds.

Alicia and Jo walked part of the way
and skied the rest.

Alicia said:
'We were walking up frozen waterfalls
and mountains.'

They completed the journey in ten days –
one day faster than her father had done it!

Alicia's father said he was very proud,
but slightly upset that she'd
done it faster than him.
'But she had much better
skis than I have got,' he said.

Alicia and her father, celebrating reaching the North Pole.

Endnote – Small World

These are just a few of the people
who have made great journeys.
Other people have sailed around the world –
like Claire Francis.

Or run seven marathons in seven continents –
like Sir Ranulph Fiennes.

There are people who have climbed mountains.
People who have marched through jungles.

It's a big world –
but in another way,
it's a small world.
You can reach any part of it,
if you are brave, and strong,
and want to enough.

If *you* could make any journey in the world,
where would you go?